# STONES AND STARS

*Stones and Stars*
First published by The Dedalus Press, 2013
The Dedalus Press
13 Moyclare Road
Baldoyle
Dublin 13
Ireland

www.dedaluspress.com

This volume brings together poems first pubished in two original Dedalus Press publications, *The Absent Fountain* (1992) and *These Black Stars* (2003).

Copyright © Paul Murray, 1992, 2003, 2013

ISBN 978 1 906614 71 3

All rights reserved.
No part of this publication may be reproduced in any form or by any means without the prior permission of the publisher.

Dedalus Press titles are represented in the UK by Central Books, 99 Wallis Road, London E9 5LN and in North America by Syracuse University Press, Inc., 621 Skytop Road, Suite 110, Syracuse, New York 13244.

Cover image: 'The Falling Stars'
from Hildegard of Bingen's *Illuminations.*

The Dedalus Press receives financial assistance from
The Arts Council / An Chomhairle Ealaíon

# STONES AND STARS

## Paul Murray

DEDALUS PRESS
DUBLIN, IRELAND

*To Patrick Pye*

# Contents

### THE ABSENT FOUNTAIN (1992)

#### FIRST VOICES

The Absent Fountain / 13
'Know Thyself' / 14
Night Thought / 15
Let us Pray for the Living / 16
The Cry / 17
Steel / 18
The Ascent of Love / 19
The Awareness / 20
Threshold / 21
The Shining / 22
The Distant Pier / 23
The First Wisdom / 24
The Moment / 25
The Teachers / 26
A Short Prayer / 27
What Hope Is / 28
On Turning the Other Cheek / 29
A Note on Human Passion / 30
Seasons / 31

#### THE TESTAMENT OF MOLING

Ego Scriptor / 35
A Warning / 36
Statement / 37
The Happiness of Moling / 38

O God my God  /  40
Lightning  /  41
The Exegete  /  42
Rubrics  /  43
The Bird Man  /  44
In Extremis  /  45


OTHER VOICES

The Death-Poem of St Ciaran  /  49
Ulster Relics  /  50
The Art of Poetry  /  52
The Shell  /  54
The Poet's Love  /  55
The Mystery of Eros  /  56
A Song for the Sage  /  58


HOMAGE TO THE VOID

Homage to the Void  /  63
Cloud  /  64
The Unmanifest  /  65
Angel of the Void  /  66
The Poem of Non-Being  /  68
The Healing  /  69
Phoenix  /  70
The Fable of Being  /  71
Invocation  /  73
The Question  /  74
On Living Life to the Full  /  75
Out in the Open  /  76
The Canticle of the Void  /  77

## THESE BLACK STARS (2003)

### PART ONE

In the Making  /  89
The Seagulls in the City  /  90
The Wall Fountain  /  92
The Gap  /  93
Eriugena in Old Age  /  94
Voice and Shadow  /  96
At the Edge  /  97
A Song for the Afflicted  /  98
The Sign  /  99
Death is No Stranger  /  100
Between  /  101
The Sun Tree  /  102

### PART TWO

The Witnesses  /  107
Insight  /  108
Invisible Storm  /  109
Lines for Natasha  /  110
The Delay  /  111
The Red Hand  /  112
Your Life  /  113
At the Year's End  /  114
A Journey Within  /  115
The Knowledge of Good and Evil  /  117
The Gift  /  118
Tell us, Poet  /  119
In the End  /  120

## Part Three

The Second-Youngest / 123
Days and Nights / 125
Bewilderment / 126
A Surprise / 127
A Note in the Margin / 128
What Remains / 129
The Space Between / 130
Meteor / 131
The Breath, the Clay / 132
Mind and Heart / 134
The Shining Canto / 135
Waiting on God / 136

## Part Four

The Return / 141
Night Wind / 142
Hope / 143
Stones and Stars / 144
The Source / 145
A Glance, A Word / 146
Nocturnal / 147
The Rock / 148
Rising / 149
Beginning / 150

## THE ABSENT FOUNTAIN

The apparent absence of God in this world
is the actual reality of God.
— Simone Weil

# First Voices

## The Absent Fountain

*'To him who is dying of thirst the absent fountain, for all its absence, is nevertheless sweeter than were a world in which there were no fountains.'*
— Antoine de Saint-Exupery

My soul
was dry, and dry
as dust
lay the roots
of my awareness.

I had almost
forgotten you were alive.

But like
the sea-spray
or like the rising
spray
of a fountain

your absence
grazed my lips
and left its freshness
falling
through the air.

## 'Know Thyself'

There is a world within you
    no one has ever seen,
a voice no one has ever heard,
    not even you.
As yet unknown
    you are your own seer,
your own interpreter.
    And so, with eyes and ears
grown sharp for voice or sign,
    listen well —
not to these words
    but to that inward voice,
that impulse beating in your heart
    like a far wave.
Turn to that source, and you
    will find
what no one has ever found,
    a ground within you
no one has ever seen,
    a world beyond the limits
of your dream's horizon.

## Night Thought

Between the stars
there will be no peace,
between the islands
no rest

until the eyes
of the smallest creatures
reach
to the far-off Pleiades

and the shadow
that falls
between moment and moment
is lost in the sun.

## Let us Pray for the Living

In their rites of passage,
in their crossings,
the dead — like us —
need love, need courage:
Let us pray for the dead.

And remember, remember
those who have been grazed
by the tip of death's wing
and feel the heart naked:
Let us pray for the living.

# The Cry

When I awoke, the room was dark
    and the rain was beating
against the window pane.
    It was the room that faces out to sea,
the room in which I was born.

And from my bed I thought I saw
    the dark curtains lifting
and moving, and thought I heard
    far out at sea
a lone seabird crying in the storm.

But, as I listened, there leaned
    against my heart
— and it made me tremble — the memory
    of that other dream,
the same dream, that other night.

And I thought to myself: Is it
    possible, then,
I am not awake at all, and the rain
    is not now beating
against the window pane

And there is no seabird crying
    in the storm,
but that, instead, once more,
    this stark
isolated cry is, perhaps, my own?

## Steel

Words heard on the lips of memory
— or one word even, one single word,
how much more powerful
it is than jarring talk,
how clear and resonant!
                                    But think now
how like a blade of steel one word
can prise open the heart.

## The Ascent of Love

Your heart, you say,
has been twisted
now this way, now that.
You say you can bear it
no longer.
But soon, I suspect,
when you have climbed
the steep and jagged
layers and crevices
of feeling,
soon you will surprise
yourself, and say:
'So what if I have had
great bitterness: Am I
not glad — not thankful
the ropes
of my heart's blood
are not ropes of sand?'

## The Awareness

This
is my fear, this
my desire:

the naked, simple awareness
— like a flame —
of all that is not myself

the wound
of the knowledge of being.

## Threshold

Not at the pointed
hour of ecstasy
nor at the furthest edge
of being,
but here, in the even
close-knit hours
among the weekday
goings-on
of wind and weather,
here is our hidden threshold
of perception,
here we must wait
until the doors of the present
swing open
on new hinges.

## The Shining

A radiance — like gossamer —
yet thinner
        even than a thread
in a spider's web.

Where is it now?
Where has it gone?

## The Distant Pier

How it is that words then said
and silences we kept
on that occasion have given
shape and meaning to my solitude
I cannot explain.

It was late in the afternoon,
I remember,
and we were walking at our ease
back and forth
on the grey, granite pier
near Ostia Antica,
with then, as now, only
the sound of your words
— not the shape, not the meaning
distinct in my ear.

But those words, your words,
remain like music in my solitude,
and the sound of your voice
is like clear water lapping
and breaking
against the prow of my mind.

## The First Wisdom

Beautiful
are the texts of the Masters,
luminous and practical
their teaching.

But for me
more useful still,
my best-thumbed pages
of enlightenment

and the text and title
of my greatest learning,
are my own
faults and failings.

## The Moment

This moment,
the grace of this one, raptureless
moment
is the place of pilgrimage
to which I am a pilgrim.

## The Teachers

There are three faces of the Self
each one of us conceals:
the silent fool, the subtle dreamer
and the suffering child.

But what is their importance?
What have they to teach
beyond the duties and desires,
the pleasures and pieties of living?

They teach us to survive.

## A Short Prayer

Be near us, Lord,
when words of trust are broken
and all we know of brightness
has died.

When words of friends, and even
our own words, like waves
of the sea, prove transitory
and hazardous,

Be near us, Lord,
be our integrity.

## What Hope Is

You think you know despair
and think you know
what hope is. But think again:
remember the hidden tenderness
of men and women
down on their knees today
to wash and dress
the leprous wounds of those
who will not walk tomorrow.

## On Turning the Other Cheek

Love's
vengeance is mercy:

how else
explain the blow that is
not returned

but instead
is constrained
by a love
more fierce than death

and with
a shuddering thrust
of pain
and of tenderness

is aimed
at the heart.

## A Note on Human Passion

Sacred or profane
— it does not matter —
one must not anaesthetize
or dull the pain
but instead sustain
the splintered heart's
helpless yet terrifying
and sharp desire
never to be healed
of the wound of living.

## Seasons

In quick or in slow succession, frost
into fire, fire into frost,
the seasons of the year return
and leave us numb with cold
or warm us, like the seasons of the heart.

But that last season you endured
— your heart's dark winter —
was so bleak and cold that still
to this day, to this hour,
the frost remains in your blood.

But now is the moment of change,
now the apocalypse.
Today, swept by the winds of another
season, the blossoms
of the fruit trees are ablaze with colour.

Surely it is the end of spring,
the promised summer?
So say 'yes' and 'yes' again
to this moment
while it turns, for soon it will be gone.

And soon the trees of spring
will become the trees of memory,
and will be shaken by the powerful winds
of memory, cowering
like blown candles and blazing askew.

## The Testament of Moling

The poems in this sequence are 'voiced' for Moling, an Irish monk and poet of the seventh century. Although in part inspired by traditional legends the poems are not based directly on any surviving fragments composed by Moling himself. One poem, 'The Bird Man: Homage to Sweeney Astray', refers to the poet Mad Sweeney, an outcast befriended by Moling.

## Ego Scriptor

Steep
is the path before me
and dark the issue.
The time for mere words
is over.

Yet here am I
still trying
to compose
in this bright margin
one lean poem.

## A Warning

Begin as you wish
and pursue
your own line of thought
or feeling;
but be prepared
to be surprised.

Sometimes,
within the first word
of a sentence,
or in the first letter
of a word,
are loops and turns.

And almost every scribe
or learned copyist
has seen
        — emerging
from the green
innocence of a tree —

the most lovely
curve of thought
or arc
of feeling
slowly uncoil itself
into a serpent.

# Statement

To be, for weeks, the glad
disciple of a single thought
has left me dazed
yet happy as a thrush.
It is the thought that
He, giver of the gifts we bring,
He who needs nothing
has need of us, and that
if you or I should cease to be,
He would die of sadness.

## The Happiness of Moling

Contented in both quiet
and disquiet I was
a saint without a halo,

shattered and yet happy,
winning
on a losing hand,

saving my own
and others' lives
daily and hourly.

*

Force-fed by need,
fulfilled
by hunger,

I became
a beggar among beggars
and became a god,

dependant on that love
which feeds
on its own bestowal,

asking for no gifts
and thus
receiving them hourly.

*

Learning, first,
not to expect
too much

and, later,
not to expect
anything at all.

## O God my God

You have slain me
with the sword of quiet

and in my blood again
that stillness

as if the throb of life itself
had paused.

## Lightning

In the fissure of the moment,
in the sudden lightning
of God's mercy

the saint
is indistinguishable
from the sinner,

and the flowers of earth
and the flowers of heaven
are the same.

## The Exegete

More head than heart
more pride than sense,
I tried to sift
God's word like wheat,
hungered
for absolute corn.
It was a pointless task —

Since, with the vain
and with the vulgar,
God has shared his bread
and, through his poets
and his saints, has said:
'To me
nothing human is alien'.

# Rubrics

*'With my body I thee worship'*

The statement of love a man
makes to his bride
and a bride to her husband
is their pure gift of trust,
and is the form that love takes
in our worship of God.

And thus we are at ease
with our desire to pray,
yet cannot rest in prayer
and cannot love
until we give ourselves entire,
body, mind and soul —
passionate in ritual
as in the gestures of love
and passionate
in the control of gesture:

The act of obeisance, done
with reverence, and always
according to the ancient
rubrics prescribed
by the laws of the blood
which are the laws
of the book: the entire rite
performed — more, nearly,
than almost any other
activity — for its own sake.

# The Bird Man

*Homage to Sweeney Astray*

Pity the mad poet
— never —
he will despise your pity.

But rather
envy him his madness:

he who has climbed
like a stray thrush
far into the sky

who has brushed with his wings
and caught
in his hand like a sword

the white pain
arrows of white stars
forked lightning.

## In Extremis

Between
my body and my soul
an armistice
hangs by a thread.

I can still live. I can still
breathe.

My limbs,
my arms and my legs,
like sticks
glued to my body

and my heart's blood
chilled by fears
yet roused and giddy
with enchantment and remorse

still red
as a wild rowan berry!

**Other Voices**

# The Death-Poem of St Ciaran

St Ciaran spoke to his monks at Clonmacnoise concerning a great and terrible disaster which, 'towards the end of the world', would be visited upon their monastic city. His monks then asked him: 'What shall we do at that time, stay here by your relics or go elsewhere?' Ciaran replied:

>Bury my bones
>on the side of a hill
>like the stag's.
>
>And do not bow down
>before my relics
>but be inspired by my spirit.

## Ulster Relics

It would be madness
to strip the orange from the lily.
Long live the orange!

It would be madness
to peel the green from the fields.
Long live the green!

But to strip our minds of prejudice,
to tear up with our hands
the painted flags of prejudice
and pull down
those coloured rags and relics,

that is not madness.

*

For too long now, for too long already,
we have paraded our relics
before us
and have ourselves become like
                                   relics
— tainted and stained, yet still righteous
in display, and worn yearly —
like faded relics of the past.

March after march,
procession after procession after procession.

Our drums beat out their news
our bands proclaim
the green or the black or the orange.
But to what end, to what purpose?
What can our drums explain,
what can they excuse
if, in the end, we kneel to tribal
gods, but are unworthy
of our own children, nursing prejudice
even at the breast, and breeding
guilt and hatred with religious milk?

Our drums beat out their news.
March after march,
procession after procession after procession.

# The Art of Poetry

I

Say what you will,
though the desire seem crazy,
the gift is not distinct
from the desire,
and you must try
to shape out of their cloth
a timeless, woven music.
And even if the strands
of thought,
the threads of imagery you use,
have with rare love and ease
by other hands been drawn,
today, it is your weave,
your love, these threads obey —
though still
through time unravelling.

II

As the slow wheel of language turns
and as the brilliant loom
of thought and of emotion changes,
gradually, slowly,
these newly-borrowed images and forms,
these stolen traces,
these hooked, half-conscious memories
of theme and phrase, are now
being drawn into the very warp and woof,
woven into the cadence
of your own heart's music.

## The Shell

Even as I held it,
as I turned it slowly round
in my hands,
it changed from gold to grey:
the dream shell.

So I threw it away
upon the sand in irritation.
But a wave
came out of the sea
and filled it.

And, choking and gasping
for air, I woke out of sleep
and turned in my bed
as the curved shell turned
in its bed in the sea.

And awake from the dream
the whorl in the shell of my being
was filled — at that instant —
with rapture,
wave upon wave!

## The Poet's Love

Let's face it:
the poet's love is suspect.

Even the creatures and dreams
he has woven
out of the silk of need

do not know if they are graced
or cursed
to have been formed under his fingers.

## The Mystery of Eros

When I hear you breathe,
your spirit is like the wind's,
it is like the tide's.

Your spirit has its laws
but it has no rules.

Magician of the fabulous,
conjuror from nowhere
of pink and red desires,
of white doves of thought,
of scarves the colour of pain
and hope,
what is your secret?

*

When the sun rises
or the moon fades
the most penetrable gaze
is yours and thus
the most penetrating.

But will you bring me
death
or bring me
life?
I should know you by now.

The sound
of your approaching step,
the clamour in my heart
that is awakened
by your merest footfall.

## A Song for the Sage

Not that flame
— the known desire —
but another
flame's tongued fire
has found
and frightened me,
has burned
out of the void
and devoured
my mind and senses.

    *

If only I could
have glimpsed it
once

no more than that

glimpsed it
in passing
and then forgotten

it would have been enough.

    *

If only I could
have seen
how terrible it was

how dangerous
to be so near
the flame

so near
the fierce lip
of its burning

the flame
not of desire
but of its absence.

## Homage to the Void

While it is silent, it calls out and while it calls out it is silent; and the invisible is seen and while it is seen, it remains invisible.
— John Scotus Eriugena

# Homage to the Void

The first glimpse
of you — I remember —
was of something perilous
yet lovely.
You were like a source
that had no beginning,
like a spring welling up
in the eyes of oblivion.
And so perilous you seemed
and so intolerably lovely
I thought to myself:
'It is a dream
it is no more than that'.

But what a weight of absence
— O Nameless One —
as you leaned against me
suddenly
like a wall of air,
as you stared into my eyes
and stared through me,
your eyes and gaze
incurious
yet all-perceiving,
your dark eyes
like the closed wings
of a dreaming butterfly.

## Cloud

It does not
rain. Or,
if it rains, it rains only
out of a sky
that does not yet exist.

And always,
without our knowing it,
our hands
and lips and eyes
are lulled awake

by the moistures
of the cloud
of non-being.

## The Unmanifest

Obscure and dark
as ever, yet
leaving, as it does,
every form
every gesture shining
as it passes,
I had thought
the illumination
of our time
would make it visible.

But it is plain sense
to me now
that, immanent
though it is
and radiant,
this ray
of darkness,
this torch of the void
cannot be proven
nor yet disproven.

## Angel of the Void

How long will your vigil last?

You peer at us
from stars behind stars.

So near to us
and yet so far remote.

    \*

There is no nakedness
more terrible than yours
no look, no touch,
no touch —
none, none in all the world
that so inflames
my pulse, that burns
so deep
a space within my soul.

    \*

At your approach
the bright gods on their pedestals
began to shiver

and I also trembled.

You were like a mirror
with your face of glass
turned towards me

with your mouth
and eyes of quicksilver.

     *

Was it yours
that unseen hand which raised
the gleaming sword
at our creation

and pierced our side
and scarred us
with this staunchless wound
this helpless longing?

# The Poem of Non-Being

Without
that cloud of
absence

around us

without
these drops of
cool sound

how else
could there
rain down on us

the knowledge
that we might
never have been?

# The Healing

When the rigid pendulum
falters, and you feel the void,
like nerves, like blood,
begin to permeate your being,
do not be afraid. It is not
ecstasy and the joy of living
it would destroy, but rather
death and the thraldom of death,
the slow swooning away
from the actual,
the lust for oblivion.

# Phoenix

It is within these eyes
(O cruel blindness!
O burning nest of mirrors!)
it is within these eyes:
what the self cannot know
what the far crest of being cannot see
when it stops
when it turns back
and looks at itself.

It is within these eyes
(O pupil of unawareness!
O gaze of absence!)
that the scorched, imperishable
wings of the phoenix
are opening, and the freed void
rises above a blaze of suns
and death
burns into silence.

# The Fable of Being

I have heard it again
echoing and singing
out of nowhere
that small
hum-note
calling and calling
like an ancient hymn.

*

'Come,' it sings,
and the echo
of its voice in my ear
sings: 'Come,
whoever you are. See
where creation's weights
and wheels are held.
Come now to where
each sliding hour,
each form
recalls its silent origin.
Here where you stand
the youngest light
and the oldest darkness
are beginning to mingle.'

*

When I looked, I saw
rising
above the waters of the void

a star of the impossible.
And in my eyes it shone
and in my soul
like the appearance of Now
like the existence of Yes.

## Invocation

O void
tear open the sky!

Rip it apart
like a used page,
a frayed garment.

Tear it to pieces!

      *

O let your forked
lightning
raise fire in our dust.
Let it flame
on these graves.
Let it strike
at our veins of death.

# The Question

Midnight.
All is silent.

Yet still the question
of the void
amazes the stars.

## On Living Life to the Full

When your heart is empty
and your hands are empty

you can take into your hands
the gift of the present

you can experience in your heart
the moment in its fullness.

*

And this you will know,
though perhaps you may not yet
understand it,

this you will know:

that nothing
of all you have longed for
or have sought to hold fast
can relieve you of your thirst,
your loneliness,

until you learn
to take in your hands
and raise to your lips
this cup of solitude
this chalice of the void

and drain it to the dregs.

## Out in the Open

Falling like a scimitar
or like a bolt of lightning
the arrow of the void
has struck its mark.

And in a sudden wave
of heat and freshness

I am drenched through
with the joy of being alive!

# The Canticle of the Void

Smaller than the small
I am that still centre
within you
that needle's eye
through which all the threads
of the universe are drawn.

Perhaps you think you know me
but you do not know me.

Of everything that is,
of every word that is spoken
on the lips
or in the heart,
of every thought and hope and wish,
I am the silent witness.

*

Nearer to you than ecstasy
in the blood
yet more mysterious far

I am the guardian
of every colour
that catches the eye,
of every taste
that pleases the tongue,
of every word
that speaks to the heart.

*

Perhaps you think you know me
but you do not know me.

Mine is the voice
that sings out of the voiceless
night, that rises
like music out of the root
of the dark thorn, out of the lucid
throat of the fountain.

*

Smaller than the small

I am the seed
of all that is known
and unknown.

I am the root
and stem of meaning,
the ground

of wonder. Through me,
each leading
tendril of desire

is drawn,
and breathes in
consciousness of Being.

*

And yet when you open
your ears to my voice
and listen with all your hearing
and listen again,
no subtle joining of notes and words,
no vertical song is heard

but silence is singing.

And when you open your eyes
to my appearance
but cannot see me,
or when you close your eyes
and close your ears in concentration
and look with your hands
and turn back again the pages
of sleep's dark scripture,
no great or terrible sign awakes,
no vision burns

but absence is shining.

*

Mine is the secret
that lies hidden
like the lustrous pearl

gleaming
within its oyster

the deepest secret,
the secret
hidden within the secret.

# THESE BLACK STARS

*To my Mother*

Breath
gone from your lips.
Your hand in mine,
a stilled branch.


*To my Father*

The sound of your voice
more faint than ever now
still beating in my pulse
like a tin drum in a dream.

There are times of suffering which remain in our lives like black absolutes, and are not blotted out. Fortunate are those for whom these black stars shed some sort of light.
— Iris Murdoch

*Part One*

## In the Making

The gift, when it comes,
comes always from where
you least expect: either
from that hurt void you feel
after actual loss
or from the mere absence
of a longed-for music,
from a line or a theme
you cannot seem to recall
or a phrase of a poem
you cannot complete.
But then with an instinct
born from that lack
or that need – suddenly,
out of the side
of the poem, another music
begins, another song.
And there it is on its feet,
bone of your bone and yet
free, flesh of your flesh
but not yours, a theme
like a new Eve emerging.

## The Seagulls in the City

Bizarre
that you pursue me
this far out of the past,
                       arriving
in groups of two or three
on the wing,
            gliding
above the roof-tops,
and at all hours,
                    night and morning,
salting the air with your cries.

                \*

Useless
to pretend it could be different.
It cannot.
        For always
and almost against
my will
            something in my blood
wakens at the surprise of
your trespass,
                  something in my pulse
responds
to the strong, dream-like insistence
of your appearing.

                \*

At times it is enough
for me
        and for the earth-bound
if your wings tilt
downward
        even a little.
For in that instant,
        as the mind
turns on its axis and small wings
of desire
        begin to veer
back into the past,
it is as if the whole world
                were tilting
sideways into the wind.

# The Wall Fountain

*(La Fontanella del Facchino, Rome)*

    Do not be surprised
if he is still there at the corner
of your thoughts, as once
    at the corner of your street:
the man of stone, that sad
exhausted man who leans out
    from the wall fountain
still holding in his marble hands
a barrel of stone that leaks
    water like time.
And do not be amazed
if you can still hear the sound
    that wakes in you
so many memories. Listen
and listen deep and well. Then
    let them pass.
For in or near this place
you love, this source, you cannot
    stop or trap the water
as it spills, or keep these days
and hours, these weeks and months
    from being poured away.

# The Gap

I try, even now,
when the cold wind
blows through each sense

to close the door.

But hard though
I try, never have I
learned to hold firm

once and for all

the uneasy, loosening
hinge between
sense and thought.

## Eriugena in Old Age

So many loops and bends has
this familiar path
it can still surprise me.

Sometimes it is like a
small child running up ahead
in the darkness.

*

But is it a path
that is real, this climbing path
that draws me away
from the most near and most visible:

my mind released,
as never before, by negation
of the obvious,
my five senses blurred

and the eyes and ears
of my soul enthralled,
as never before, by their perception
of the unseen and the unheard?

*

This climbing path, my mind's path,
now draws me away
from the care of this hour

and from the hub of a small world
of hours and minutes —
but is it a path that is real?

## Voice and Shadow

Your voice at birth,
a gull-screech.
Your last breath,
the shadow of a sea-bird
on the vast waters.

## At the Edge

No, there are no words,
there is no image to describe it,
the music of enchantment!

But, later, when the
notes of the song die out
one after another — 'the sweet cheat gone'—
what's left?
　　　　　Thoughts
at the edge of thought, hard-bitten,
crystalline.
　　　　　And no tremor
in the veins, no easy
rhythm of a woven music
　　　　　　　　　　but words
on the page, packed
with hurt and rapture.

## A Song for the Afflicted

*'To go to hell one need change
neither one's place nor one's position.'*
— Rafael Alberti

This hell
has the sadness of pain
that cannot cry.
It is lodged
beneath the skin
beneath the mask.
It is a thing
that gnaws at being,
like a worm.
In this hell there is
no fire to feel, no flame
that stirs, no sound.
Yet — whose is that fire
within, that voice
which burns, and sings:
Hidden within the deepest
self — no matter how
treacherous one has been
or how corruptible — hidden
within the deepest self
the seed of love remains.

## The Sign

    Yes, an uncommon hurt
though common in its source, a wounded
trust, an anguish felt for years.
    But what you have endured
of pain, the ways you have been
scarred, has etched a sign so deep
    it still appals.
Not the marks on a saint's body
those tiny, wounded stars
    on feet and hands
but the dark stigmata your name
and flesh received from the thongs
    and spears of rumour.
Sometimes I think
a brand on the forehead — like Cain's —
    would have been less cruel.

## Death is no Stranger

To the living it is a well
of fear, a hidden
font of oil from which is fed
                             the flame
that burns
under all our thoughts, under all
our gestures.
               At times
it can appear like love itself
                             so real
as almost to keep us alive —
To the living, death is no stranger.

# Between

Somehow it is enough, after
the day's long weariness of paths
and detours, if suddenly
                         a bird
calls in the stillness
and, between its clear
                         sharp summons
and your own heart, you hear
even the smallest silence.

## The Sun Tree

Light, the last
of the light of day: look
at its branching form

how it spreads
like fire from the opposite
shore to where you stand,

a light so near you now,
so strong,
it draws your gaze

it lifts your thoughts up
into its branches,
into its nest of hope,

and holds you
there, and holds its ground
as if with shape

undimmed, with trunk
unbowed, it weighs
and flames against your loss.

Is it a sign? Is it
a blessing? You have not
asked for a sign

and there are no words
left. But blazing now,
and ending,

with all its myriad
leaves on fire, its wood
aflame, look how it dips

and sways on the water
as if, merely
by shining, to answer

the cold and the dark.

*Part Two*

## The Witnesses

Already we had surged
    forward with the rest
        onto the bus

making it in just in time
    before the doors slammed
        shut behind us

but not in time to
    catch the stone
        brooch which sprang

from your dress and spun
    out through the doors
        like a tiny

stunned universe — all of us
    together on the bus
        staring after it

in amazement as if we were
    for that instant
        the astonished witnesses

of a first rock being hurled
    out into existence
        after the Big Bang!

## Insight

As bright, as
sudden
       as the leap of
a grasshopper
            glimpsed
in a field of vision —

how swift
how extraordinary!

## Invisible Storm

    It has not passed
through me, not yet, not passed
completely, the escaping
    tumult and its portent
still held within my senses.
What was it that loomed
    towards me? What
was it that appeared?
Something other
    than the rain, other
than the sound of the wind
coming in from the sea.
    But was I not
asleep, and wakened from
my sleep by the stirring
    of the sea wind
and the distant thunder?
And am I not
    remembering again
the first sharp breaking-in
of vision on my world,
    that storm
of hands at dusk, shaking
the huge and shining leaves?

## Lines for Natasha

> Natasha Tubelskaya, a celebrated artist, was still relatively young when her apartment in Rome went up in flames on 17 February, 2002.

I will not bring flowers for your grave
not even the great lilies or the dark tulips
you loved.

I will not bring plaited wreaths or sermons
or even tears. The way you died has dried
all my tears.

I will not haunt your death.

I will not try to go back again
to the scorched room where you died
or to the thought of your fear at the end.

I will not seek
– not even for your sake — to re-live
the nightmare of the dropping flames.

I will not try to prove how swift
the end came, nor will I ask again
of your last seconds.

I will make no pact with your death.

I will not shape out of loss
or try to name the meaning of that hour
which had no exit.

I will make no pact with your death.

# The Delay

    Now that the spectres
of the past, like rumours or like ghosts
of war, are drifting on every wind,
    how long must we await
your coming, Lord? Knowing so little,
destroyed by what we know, guessing
    so much and so much,
our lives, like the air itself around us,
woven with the threads of a story
    time alone can unravel.

    But you, Lord,
have you not signed the air
with your name, have you not carved it
    on our hearts with a comet's
god-like brilliancy and signature?
Why then do you remain
    remote from us, or why appear
so close yet indistinct, a radiance
unseen, a gift desired, a face, a name,
    our fingers trace in the dark?

    Now, even in our need,
when we try to pray to you, or try
to feed our minds on your presence,
    our thoughts are like words
in a dream, our prayers like crumbs
falling from the hand of sleep.
    Ah come, Lord, do not delay.
The weave and fabric of our lives
is worn: we need mending.
    Our righteousness is threadbare.

## The Red Hand

When dreams are dipped
                      in blood
and words dressed up to kill
what does it matter
                      which banner
or flag we carry
or what we're wearing — ritual
stole or sash?
                      This anger
in our bones and blood, this hatred
on our tongue, is not
                      the anger of God
but only hurt become dangerous.

## Your Life

It may be over
the wind sang — over
before you know it.

Your whole life
blurred and shaken
as this hour
that stumbles on its feet
and flaps its wings
like a jackdaw —

Then lifts and is gone.

## At the Year's End

Deliver from their
strange sadness, Lord,

those who are no longer
disturbed by love

and feel no fear, no pain,
as calmly, blandly,

they turn over the first
and last days of the year

like a coin in their pockets.

# A Journey Within

As you enter,
the door swings back
against the light

behind you
and the world flashes
like a spent bulb.

Halted by the darkness
you are scarcely
able, at first,

to understand
where it is
you have come from

or why you are here
or where it is
you are gomg.

All that is clear
all that you can
understand

is that the
long lapse of time
has made you

a stranger.
And yet, even now,
even here

as the locked door
opens
into your emptied

memory, a small
trail of silvery dust
begins to stir.

# The Knowledge of Good and Evil

       1 *The Apple*

Almost mine —
but not mine yet.
           There it hangs
just out of reach.
           Ah, if only
I could grasp it, hold it
to my lips,
it would taste so delicious.

       2  *The Surprise*

A windfall at last and no mistaking!
This is bliss, I thought, pure bliss.
I was so certain.
           Here, they said,
taste this, and again, taste this.
It is free, it is yours. Feast now
on a harvest of pleasure.

But what a sparse harvest it was,
what ghost sweetness!
From rind to core how sour
it was to taste that fallen fruit,
that unforbidden knowledge.

# The Gift

Amazing —
no matter how
tired you feel
under the chill
downpour of
a dead routine
or how your
nerves and senses
ache, it's hard
not to affirm
the thought
that even under
the malign
powers of rust
and rain, the heart
survives, the soul
retains its gift
of weathering.

## Tell us, Poet

    Tell us, poet, tell
us now, while the pulse of
colour still throbs
    in your idle veins,
what is the test of
love? How can we know
    if the dazed
instant, the moving circle
of enchantment
    on which we turn,
the moment's
live, unstoppable wheel,
    will burn out
under the weight of loss
or — under the force of
    love — burn on and on?

## In the End

That they know it
or not, that we
know it or not
is not important.
What matters is
that all of us, all
of them, lovers
and madmen, mothers
and sad men — all
sing from a wound.

*Part Three*

## The Second Youngest

My hair still dripping wet
after the bath and with, at last,
the large white towel which had
hung over my shoulders
now in his hands
I thought, as I knelt on the ground
before my father
and he dried my hair and talked,
I was the son of a god.

It was the same
warmth, the same repeated ritual
for all of us — my four brothers
and my three sisters —
when, in turn, after our bath
we would climb
the dark stairs to the lighted room
where my father sat in his chair.

We were, I suppose, like small
initiates: the girls
in their coloured night-gowns
and red slippers, and the boys
with our white towels
across our shoulders, wearing pyjamas
but naked from the waist up.

No pilgrims of the Absolute,
it's clear, no shining devotees
in saffron ever looked
as radiant and cleansed as we did

or ever climbed
to their illumined states of soul
as we climbed up those stairs!

I was five or at most
six years old, the second youngest.
But once I had
braved the darkness of the stairs
alone, my trial was over.
From shadows into light
the door opened, and I stepped
into the hush of the room.

So vivid, I remember, that bright
threshold! But real
illumination came, moments
later, when I knelt down
next to the fire, as near
as I could to my father's chair,
and bowed my head.

I remember, as soon
as he began to dry my hair
with the towel
and warm my hair with his hands
lifting his two palms
to the fire
and letting them rest on my head,

I thought I was the son of a god.

## Days and Nights

All that's over now, you say,
all past and gone — and I agree.
   But wise men, wise women
of my generation, can you tell me
where they have gone, the days
   and nights of childhood,
where they are now? Have they
got lost within the loop of time?
   Are they in hiding?
Will they, if I learn their game,
if I take my hands away
   from my eyes, will they
come tumbling back from behind
the years? Wise men, wise women
   of my generation, tell me:
where are they now,
the days and nights of childhood,
   where have they gone?

## Bewilderment

To the child's
first conscious gaze
or to the troubled seer

how utterly
wonderfully strange

the way time
loads our days with gifts,
with dangers —

how handsomely
it draws its fateful
circle around us.

## A Surprise

    Scandalous,
no doubt, but a sign also
of a latent faithfulness
    in things

    and in us
of a surviving trust.
For though they blush
    scarlet

    with shame,
roses, clasped in the hand
or splayed in the arms of a hypocrite,
    remain beautiful.

## A Note in the Margin

Amazing how
they seem to make sense
of us, though we

cannot
make sense of them,
those alarming

coincidences in our lives,
those rare
gestures of meaning

like twin
heads, facing each other
on the page,

eyeball to eyeball.

## What Remains

If love is stronger
than death, will even
these, our pillaged

lives, our dreams,
one day be restored
like fragments

of a broken song?
Or will they
be changed under

some hand,
transformed like gathered
bits of wood

and coloured stone,
small fragments saved
from tumbled

walls we knew, from
stairs and vanished floors
and rooms?

# The Space Between

*I said: 'God. I want freedom in salvation'.*
— Arthur Rimbaud


What happened was for me
a kind of miracle

like being suddenly able
to breathe under water

the astonishment at finding
it possible again to believe

and at finding the space
to breathe and breathe deep

between the word 'freedom'
and the word 'God'.

## Meteor

No matter
that it gleams, as
always, for a second

only, or for a
hundredth of a second,
the silent

meteor
of your glance, when it
passes near, recalls

a light
that shone from before
the beginning,

a radiance that broke upon
the stillness
like a wish formed.

## The Breath, the Clay

    Unrecognisable
to anyone
but you, with your
    observant eye

    with your obsessive
love and craft,
the mystery we are,
    the actual mix

    of breath
and clay each one
is made of
    or made from.

    Our lives, our
loves, are mortal,
yes, but we are
    each one

    made in your
likeness. Our flesh,
our clay, formed
    in the unseen

    image of the
eternal Word, in the
dreamed likeness
    of the Son

      who would take
flesh. We are each one
formed in that image.
    Our spirit,

    the breath
in our souls and in
our lungs, like the breath
    of a god.

## Mind and Heart

The mind
may hold to its aim
but who will

persuade the heart
of the mind's ideal,
its impossible

possible prayer:
never again to
lust after dreams

or to allow the
hurt of the past
unhinge

the real world?

# The Shining Canto

Out of the night sky
a swarm of hiving stars
has entered my blood.

Their fallen light
has pierced me through
like a dying meteor.

Their alien
brilliance moves
along my veins

like fire.
They have burned
my lips and brow

so that I cannot sleep
for pleasure
in my blood

nor keep
a vigil now
unless that other

light, that nearer
fire, that other love
awakes.

# **Waiting on God:** *Four Songs for the Bride*

*'I sought Him whom my soul loves;
I sought Him but found Him not'.*
      — The Song of Songs 3:1

### 1. THE WAITING

When, when will it come,
will it ever come, the moment
of ease, the arrested moment

when, through one urgent
wound of peace, your love
is known, your 'toil of grace',

and particle by particle
the fiery dust in my brain
begins to settle?

### 2. O SLEEPING LORD

If I could touch
my lips to this song
as to an icon

perhaps the pressure
of my lips
the music of my song

would wound your heart
and rouse you
from your sleep.

3. INVOCATION

Like the flame that
survives until morning
and leaps upward
above the wood that it
consumes, may the spark
of this love survive
and may the flame
which absence kindles
not be put out.


4. SONG

So dark it was that night
when you came
near to me, so near
and with such love,
I could not find one word
to say but let fear
lean on love as you came
near, so near you came,
so near and with such love.

*Part Four*

## The Return

Still wondering if
the full spring will come
but happy in the
knowledge my mind's dull
winter has passed

here I am in its wake

watching my
own thoughts fly in
under the leaf
and shadow of a young
idea, dipping and

swerving like swallows.

# Night Wind

What is it
you are thinking of at night

when lying in your room
wide-awake

you can still hear though faintly
above the noise of the traffic

the night wind
coming in from the sea

whispering and humming to herself
like an ancient sorceress

and you know then
her burden of days is lifted

and the waves of the sea,
their hollows

filled with the night,
are at last beginning to ebb —

what is it you are thinking of?

# Hope

Now, before the rains
prodigal of loneliness
and desire return, lift up
your eyes if you can,
raise them to the sun.
Let your thoughts
dare to imitate the swans,
those white birds you saw
lifting themselves up
noisily from the ponds
of childhood, and lean
with them, lean
as your hope lifts to the sun
far out into the wind.

## Stones and Stars

    Always a cause
of wonder for me is how, after
hours of dull weather, days
    of drizzling rain,
that small cobble-stone street
outside my window not only
    begins at last
to breathe in the clear air, it also
somehow flames
    as it revives, changing
into a lane of tiny mirrors, a field
awash with light.
    Even now, believe me,
if you were to walk out
into the street at this hour, the wet
    cobble-stones
and the four or five yellow lamps
shining above them
    and the smaller lights,
all the lit windows of the houses,
would seem at once
    as wonderful a thing
as the sight of the thin lane of sky
over your head or as the thought
    of the infinite
dark, the vast firmament itself
sowed thick as a field with stars.

## The Source

    Winds
out of the past are still
moving among the small
      grasses.

    And, nearby,
at the foot
of the Mournes, I can hear
      flowing

      out of the dark
earth, like a gift
restored, the quiet waters
      of the Shimna.

# A Glance, A Word

Not always
will the stars feed
upon your blood

nor will
the clouds, as they pass,
starve

for your
eyes to transfix them.
There is

no need
to decipher the grammar
of past

and future. Here,
now, in your own
hands, and faster

than you can read,
the page of the moment
is burning.

# Nocturnal

Under
their silence, under
their dark feathers,
                        birds,
a minor seraphim of
birds, a hive
                of tiny starlings
in a world of frost,
though sound asleep now
in the night's domain,
                        unmovlng
in the icy cold,
            still keep
the notes of the song,
still hold
        the dream of the
warmth of the dawn,
                        under their
eyelids, under their closed
wings.

# The Rock

First, it blocks your way
then opens it, an amazing,
improbable grace, but actual.

And the force of its weight
when it hits you — if
it hits you — marks you for life.

And there is no escape
from its hurt, though its force
weakens even as its weight

holds. And you are
struck so hard, at first,
and remain so stunned

that nothing in the world,
it seems, can protect you
from its curse: that jagged

fate, that rock
against which the heart's wave
rises, live and crystalline,

and falls
and breaks most powerfully
into the foam of the spirit.

# Rising

Over the still
earth, the sun that
is rising now

is the sun
that was rising
before we were born

and will be rising
after we are dead.
And we, too, as it

dawns, revive. For
even as these
mists and fears

recede, shining now
above the dark
earth of the mind,

above the void,
three stars within us
rise, three

moving suns: passion,
wakefulness, joy.
And can such living

flame, such radiance
be born from dust
to return to dust?

## Beginning

Now, after a long night
of stillness and longing,
on my brow, in the
tiny furrows of my palm,
thin lines of dew
are forming. And what I
had despaired of so long
is here. The sun,
true to its vow, with
prophecies of light and air
wakes the horizon.
I have come through
after all. I have a new
dawn on my shoulders.

www.ingramcontent.com/pod-product-compliance
Ingram Content Group UK Ltd.
Pitfield, Milton Keynes, MK11 3LW, UK
UKHW042155190225
455331UK00001B/17